KEEP CALM, AFFIRMATIONS WORKBOOK

Positive Affirmations Workbook.
Includes: Mentoring Questions, Guidance, Supporting You.

Affirmations World

Copyright © 2019

All rights reserved. Without limiting rights under the copyright reserved above, no part of this publication may be reproduced, stored, introduced into a retrieval system, distributed or transmitted in any form or by any means, including without limitation photocopying, recording, or other electronic or mechanical methods, without the prior written permission of the publisher, except in the case of brief quotations embodied in critical reviews and certain other non-commercial uses permitted by copyright law.

The scanning, uploading, and/or distribution of this document via the internet or via any other means without the permission of the publisher is illegal and is punishable by law. Please purchase only authorized editions and do not participate in or encourage electronic piracy of copyrightable materials.

Introductory Note

Welcome to this interactive affirmations workbook which is aimed at nurturing your personal growth, develepment and improvement.

We want to start by congratulating you on this purchase. You have taken a positive step forward and invested in yourself.

This notebook & workbook has been designed to support you and your sub-conscious mind towards achieving more rewarding and positive outcomes throughout your life's journey.

The affirmations found within this workbook will benefit you greatly and we recommend mindfully repeating them regularly throughout the day - especially in the mornings and just before bed time.

You will find a series of questions & advice listed within. It is optional to follow these questions but if you find them thought provoking and useful, feel free to use them and create further positive questions for yourself. Our goal is to help you to achieve that which you desire through exploring your inner thoughts and feelings. This practice is also a form of self-therapy and journalling - let your thoughts go.

Have a great time whilst using this workbook. We trust that you will enjoy and benefit from the use of it.

Have fun and use it in the way it best serves you; become creative, draw sketches or doodles, make a note of your daily progress, brainstorm ideas & thoughts, note down daily tasks to complete or you could even use it to store memorable photos - the possibilities are endless.

Good luck and wishing you all the best.

I am full of love and contentment

I am full of love and contentment

How do you feel right now? What challenges are you currently facing and how will you overcome them? What steps can you take to improve? What Do You Feel Is Holding You Back?

_____
_____
_____
_____
_____
_____
_____
_____
_____
_____
_____
_____
_____
_____
_____
_____
_____
_____
_____

Actions You Could Take To Improve Productivity? **Be Present Minded.** New Habits You Would Like To Develop? **Feel Free To Sketch.**

I give and receive love unconditionally

I Give and Receive Love Unconditionally

How do you feel right now? What challenges are you currently facing and how will you overcome them? What steps can you take to improve? What Do You Feel Is Holding You Back?

_____

_____

_____

_____

_____

_____

_____

_____

_____

_____

_____

_____

_____

_____

_____

_____

_____

_____

_____

_____

Actions You Could Take To Improve Productivity? **Be Present Minded.** New Habits You Would Like To Develop? **Feel Free To Sketch.**

With each day that passes, I improve in every way

With Each Day That Passes, I Improve in Every Way

How do you feel right now? What challenges are you currently facing and how will you overcome them? What steps can you take to improve? What Do You Feel Is Holding You Back?

_____
_____
_____
_____
_____
_____
_____
_____
_____
_____
_____
_____
_____
_____
_____
_____
_____
_____
_____
_____
_____

Actions You Could Take To Improve Productivity? **Be Present Minded.** New Habits You Would Like To Develop? **Feel Free To Sketch.**

I learn something new daily

I Learn Something New Daily

How do you feel right now? What challenges are you currently facing and how will you overcome them? What steps can you take to improve? What Do You Feel Is Holding You Back?

_____

_____

_____

_____

_____

_____

_____

_____

_____

_____

_____

_____

_____

_____

_____

_____

_____

_____

Actions You Could Take To Improve Productivity? **Be Present Minded.** New Habits You Would Like To Develop? **Feel Free To Sketch.**

I welcome & encourage the success of others

_____

_____

_____

_____

_____

_____

_____

_____

_____

_____

_____

_____

_____

_____

I Welcome & Encourage The Success of Others

How do you feel right now? What challenges are you currently facing and how will you overcome them? What steps can you take to improve? What Do You Feel Is Holding You Back?

_____

_____

_____

_____

_____

_____

_____

_____

_____

_____

_____

_____

_____

_____

_____

_____

_____

_____

Actions You Could Take To Improve Productivity? **Be Present Minded.** New Habits You Would Like To Develop? **Feel Free To Sketch.**

I have many strengths & they are constantly expanding

_____

_____

_____

_____

_____

_____

_____

_____

_____

_____

_____

_____

_____

_____

_____

I Have Many Strengths & They Are Constantly Expanding

How do you feel right now? What challenges are you currently facing and how will you overcome them? What steps can you take to improve? What Do You Feel Is Holding You Back?

_____
_____
_____
_____
_____
_____
_____
_____
_____
_____
_____
_____
_____
_____
_____
_____
_____
_____
_____
_____

Actions You Could Take To Improve Productivity? **Be Present Minded.** New Habits You Would Like To Develop? **Feel Free To Sketch.**

I refuse to worry - I accept that I only win or learn

I Refuse To Worry - I Accept That I Only WIN or LEARN

I Refuse To Worry - I Accept That I Only Win or Learn

How do you feel right now? What challenges are you currently facing and how will you overcome them? What steps can you take to improve? What Do You Feel Is Holding You Back?

_____
_____
_____
_____
_____
_____
_____
_____
_____
_____
_____
_____
_____
_____
_____
_____
_____
_____
_____

Actions You Could Take To Improve Productivity? **Be Present Minded.** New Habits You Would Like To Develop? **Feel Free To Sketch.**

I am genuinely interested in others & their wellbeing

I am Genuinely Interested in Others & Their Wellbeing

I am Genuinely Interested in Others & Their Wellbeing

How do you feel right now? What challenges are you currently facing and how will you overcome them? What steps can you take to improve? What Do You Feel Is Holding You Back?

_____

_____

_____

_____

_____

_____

_____

_____

_____

_____

_____

_____

_____

_____

_____

_____

_____

_____

_____

Actions You Could Take To Improve Productivity? **Be Present Minded.** New Habits You Would Like To Develop? **Feel Free To Sketch.**

I deflect negative emotions (e.g. anxiety, stress, anger, sadness)

___

I Deflect Negative Emotions (e.g. Anxiety, Stress, Anger, Sadness)

How do you feel right now? What challenges are you currently facing and how will you overcome them? What steps can you take to improve? What Do You Feel Is Holding You Back?

_____

_____

_____

_____

_____

_____

_____

_____

_____

_____

_____

_____

_____

_____

_____

_____

_____

_____

_____

_____

_____

_____

Actions You Could Take To Improve Productivity? **Be Present Minded.** New Habits You Would Like To Develop? **Feel Free To Sketch.**

I only focus on positive emotions & thoughts

I Only Focus on Positive Emotions & Thoughts

I Only Focus on Positive Emotions & Thoughts

How do you feel right now? What challenges are you currently facing and how will you overcome them? What steps can you take to improve? What Do You Feel Is Holding You Back?

_____

_____

_____

_____

_____

_____

_____

_____

_____

_____

_____

_____

_____

_____

_____

_____

_____

_____

_____

Actions You Could Take To Improve Productivity? **Be Present Minded.** New Habits You Would Like To Develop? **Feel Free To Sketch.**

With each experience, I become a more refined individual

_____
_____
_____
_____
_____
_____
_____
_____
_____
_____
_____
_____
_____
_____
_____

With Each Experience, I Become a More Refined Individual

How do you feel right now? What challenges are you currently facing and how will you overcome them? What steps can you take to improve? What Do You Feel Is Holding You Back?

_____
_____
_____
_____
_____
_____
_____
_____
_____
_____
_____
_____
_____
_____
_____
_____
_____
_____
_____
_____

Actions You Could Take To Improve Productivity? **Be Present Minded.** New Habits You Would Like To Develop? **Feel Free To Sketch.**

I forgive those that hurt or upset me - past and present

I Forgive Those That Hurt or Upset Me - Past & Present

How do you feel right now? What challenges are you currently facing and how will you overcome them? What steps can you take to improve? What Do You Feel Is Holding You Back?

Actions You Could Take To Improve Productivity? **Be Present Minded.** New Habits You Would Like To Develop? **Feel Free To Sketch.**

I possess an immense positive energy

I Possess an Immense Positive Energy

How do you feel right now? What challenges are you currently facing and how will you overcome them? What steps can you take to improve? What Do You Feel Is Holding You Back?

_____
_____
_____
_____
_____
_____
_____
_____
_____
_____
_____
_____
_____
_____
_____
_____
_____
_____
_____
_____
_____

Actions You Could Take To Improve Productivity? **Be Present Minded.** New Habits You Would Like To Develop? **Feel Free To Sketch.**

I am a sincere and genuine person

I am a Sincere and Genuine Person

How do you feel right now? What challenges are you currently facing and how will you overcome them? What steps can you take to improve? What Do You Feel Is Holding You Back?

_____

_____

_____

_____

_____

_____

_____

_____

_____

_____

_____

_____

_____

_____

_____

_____

_____

_____

Actions You Could Take To Improve Productivity? **Be Present Minded.** New Habits You Would Like To Develop? **Feel Free To Sketch.**

I love every single thing about myself

I Love Every Single Thing About Myself

How do you feel right now? What challenges are you currently facing and how will you overcome them? What steps can you take to improve? What Do You Feel Is Holding You Back?

_____
_____
_____
_____
_____
_____
_____
_____
_____
_____
_____
_____
_____
_____
_____
_____
_____
_____
_____
_____

Actions You Could Take To Improve Productivity? **Be Present Minded.** New Habits You Would Like To Develop? **Feel Free To Sketch.**

I am proactive in everything I do

I am Proactive In Everything I Do

I am Proactive in Everything I Do

How do you feel right now? What challenges are you currently facing and how will you overcome them? What steps can you take to improve? What Do You Feel Is Holding You Back?

_____

_____

_____

_____

_____

_____

_____

_____

_____

_____

_____

_____

_____

_____

_____

_____

_____

_____

Actions You Could Take To Improve Productivity? **Be Present Minded.** New Habits You Would Like To Develop? **Feel Free To Sketch.**

I find happiness in every moment

I Find Happiness in Every Moment

How do you feel right now? What challenges are you currently facing and how will you overcome them? What steps can you take to improve? What Do You Feel Is Holding You Back?

_____
_____
_____
_____
_____
_____
_____
_____
_____
_____
_____
_____
_____
_____
_____
_____
_____
_____
_____
_____
_____

Actions You Could Take To Improve Productivity? **Be Present Minded.** New Habits You Would Like To Develop? **Feel Free To Sketch.**

I am persistent in everything I do

_____

_____

_____

_____

_____

_____

_____

_____

_____

_____

_____

_____

_____

I am Persistent In Everything I Do

How do you feel right now? What challenges are you currently facing and how will you overcome them? What steps can you take to improve? What Do You Feel Is Holding You Back?

Actions You Could Take To Improve Productivity? **Be Present Minded.** New Habits You Would Like To Develop? **Feel Free To Sketch.**

I am at complete peace with myself

I am Complete Peace With Myself

How do you feel right now? What challenges are you currently facing and how will you overcome them? What steps can you take to improve? What Do You Feel Is Holding You Back?

_____
_____
_____
_____
_____
_____
_____
_____
_____
_____
_____
_____
_____
_____
_____
_____
_____
_____
_____
_____

Actions You Could Take To Improve Productivity? **Be Present Minded.** New Habits You Would Like To Develop? **Feel Free To Sketch.**

I am an intelligent and focussed thinker

I am an Intelligent and Focussed Thinker

I am an Intelligent and Focussed Thinker

How do you feel right now? What challenges are you currently facing and how will you overcome them? What steps can you take to improve? What Do You Feel Is Holding You Back?

_____

_____

_____

_____

_____

_____

_____

_____

_____

_____

_____

_____

_____

_____

_____

_____

_____

_____

_____

_____

Actions You Could Take To Improve Productivity? **Be Present Minded.** New Habits You Would Like To Develop? **Feel Free To Sketch.**

I am conscious of my health and wellbeing

_____

_____

_____

_____

_____

_____

_____

_____

_____

_____

_____

_____

_____

_____

I am Conscious of my Health and Wellbeing

How do you feel right now? What challenges are you currently facing and how will you overcome them? What steps can you take to improve? What Do You Feel Is Holding You Back?

Actions You Could Take To Improve Productivity? **Be Present Minded.** New Habits You Would Like To Develop? **Feel Free To Sketch.**

I thrive on tough challenges

I Thrive on Tough Challenges

How do you feel right now? What challenges are you currently facing and how will you overcome them? What steps can you take to improve? What Do You Feel Is Holding You Back?

Actions You Could Take To Improve Productivity? **Be Present Minded.** New Habits You Would Like To Develop? **Feel Free To Sketch.**

I appreciate my life completely

I Appreciate My Life Completely

How do you feel right now? What challenges are you currently facing and how will you overcome them? What steps can you take to improve? What Do You Feel Is Holding You Back?

Actions You Could Take To Improve Productivity? **Be Present Minded.** New Habits You Would Like To Develop? **Feel Free To Sketch.**

I will continue to learn for the rest of my life

I Will Continue To Learn For The Rest Of My Life

How do you feel right now? What challenges are you currently facing and how will you overcome them? What steps can you take to improve? What Do You Feel Is Holding You Back?

_____

_____

_____

_____

_____

_____

_____

_____

_____

_____

_____

_____

_____

_____

_____

_____

_____

Actions You Could Take To Improve Productivity? **Be Present Minded.** New Habits You Would Like To Develop? **Feel Free To Sketch.**

I am courageous and have a strong presence

I am Courageous and Have a Strong Presence

How do you feel right now? What challenges are you currently facing and how will you overcome them? What steps can you take to improve? What Do You Feel Is Holding You Back?

Actions You Could Take To Improve Productivity? **Be Present Minded.** New Habits You Would Like To Develop? **Feel Free To Sketch.**

Today I drop my bad habits like they are hot coals

Today I Drop My Bad Habits Like They Are Hot Coals

How do you feel right now?
What challenges are you currently facing and how will you overcome them? What steps can you take to improve? What Do You Feel Is Holding You Back?

_____

_____

_____

_____

_____

_____

_____

_____

_____

_____

_____

_____

_____

_____

_____

_____

_____

_____

_____

Actions You Could Take To Improve Productivity? **Be Present Minded.** New Habits You Would Like To Develop? **Feel Free To Sketch.**

Every day I apply new habits that serve me positively

Every Day I Apply New Habits That Serve Me Positively

How do you feel right now? What challenges are you currently facing and how will you overcome them? What steps can you take to improve? What Do You Feel Is Holding You Back?

Actions You Could Take To Improve Productivity? **Be Present Minded.** New Habits You Would Like To Develop? **Feel Free To Sketch.**

I am unstoppable; a true powerhouse

I am Unstoppable; a True Powerhouse

I am Unstoppable: a True Powerhouse

How do you feel right now? What challenges are you currently facing and how will you overcome them? What steps can you take to improve? What Do You Feel Is Holding You Back?

_____

_____

_____

_____

_____

_____

_____

_____

_____

_____

_____

_____

_____

_____

_____

_____

_____

_____

Actions You Could Take To Improve Productivity? **Be Present Minded.** New Habits You Would Like To Develop? **Feel Free To Sketch.**

Whatever I envisage and wish for becomes a reality

Whatever I Envisage and Wish for Becomes a Reality

How do you feel right now? What challenges are you currently facing and how will you overcome them? What steps can you take to improve? What Do You Feel Is Holding You Back?

Actions You Could Take To Improve Productivity? **Be Present Minded.** New Habits You Would Like To Develop? **Feel Free To Sketch.**

I radiate charm, warmth, and generosity

I Radiate Charm, Warmth and Generosity

I Radiate Charm, Warmth and Generosity

How do you feel right now? What challenges are you currently facing and how will you overcome them? What steps can you take to improve? What Do You Feel Is Holding You Back?

Actions You Could Take To Improve Productivity? **Be Present Minded.** New Habits You Would Like To Develop? **Feel Free To Sketch.**

My thoughts are filled with positivity and compassion

_____
_____
_____
_____
_____
_____
_____
_____
_____
_____
_____
_____
_____
_____
_____
_____

My Thoughts are Filled with Positivity and Compassion

How do you feel right now? What challenges are you currently facing and how will you overcome them? What steps can you take to improve? What Do You Feel Is Holding You Back?

_____
_____
_____
_____
_____
_____
_____
_____
_____
_____
_____
_____
_____
_____
_____
_____
_____
_____
_____
_____
_____

Actions You Could Take To Improve Productivity? **Be Present Minded.** New Habits You Would Like To Develop? **Feel Free To Sketch.**

I am admired by everybody that I meet

I am Admired by Everybody that I Meet

I Admired By Everybody That I Meet

How do you feel right now? What challenges are you currently facing and how will you overcome them? What steps can you take to improve? What Do You Feel Is Holding You Back?

_____

_____

_____

_____

_____

_____

_____

_____

_____

_____

_____

_____

_____

_____

_____

_____

_____

_____

Actions You Could Take To Improve Productivity? **Be Present Minded.** New Habits You Would Like To Develop? **Feel Free To Sketch.**

Everything that happens in my life, happens for my good

_____

_____

_____

_____

_____

_____

_____

_____

_____

_____

_____

_____

_____

_____

_____

_____

Everything That Happens In My Life, Happens For My Good

How do you feel right now? What challenges are you currently facing and how will you overcome them? What steps can you take to improve? What Do You Feel Is Holding You Back?

_____

_____

_____

_____

_____

_____

_____

_____

_____

_____

_____

_____

_____

_____

_____

_____

_____

Actions You Could Take To Improve Productivity? **Be Present Minded.** New Habits You Would Like To Develop? **Feel Free To Sketch.**

Additional Notes

Made in the USA
Columbia, SC
20 December 2023